I AM
Creating My Own Experience: The Creation Vibration

by
Barry Thomas Bechta

UNCONDITIONAL
LOVE BOOKS

Redefining, Guiding, and Inspiring Humanity's
Connection to the Creative Power within.

I AM Creating My Own Experience: The Creation Vibration
by
Barry Thomas Bechta

© 2009 by BARRY THOMAS BECHTA

Library and Archives Canada Cataloguing in Publication

Bechta, Barry Thomas, 1968-
   I am creating my own experience : the creation vibration / by Barry Thomas Bechta.

ISBN 978-0-9686835-7-6

1. Self-realization--Religious aspects. I. Title.

BL624.B433 2009   204   C2009-905996-7

Publisher's Note
This publication is designed to provide accurate and authoritative information in regard to the subject matter covered. It is sold with the understanding that the author/publisher is not engaged in rendering psychological, legal, or other professional service. If advice or other assistance is required in those areas, the services of a competent professional should be sought.

I AM
Creating My
Own Experience:
The Creation Vibration

ACKNOWLEDGEMENTS

God

Ellen and Clare

Binah, Anthony, and Zac

Stephen, Margaret, Gabe, and Sam

Melinda, Paul, Sydney, and Gryphon

Every person, place, and thing in my experience

The works of these Authors and Creators: Iyanla Vanzant, Esther and Jerry Hicks with ABRAHAM, Louise L. Hay, Neale Donald Walsch, Eckhart Tolle, Dr. Wayne W. Dyer, Marianne Williamson, Jamie Sams, Dr. Norma J. Milanovich, Robert T. Kiyosaki, Alan Cohen, Mark Victor Hansen, John Randolph Price, Terry Cole-Whittaker, Richard Bach, Michael J. Losier, Richard Paul Evans, Sandra Ponder, Robert G. Allen, Og Mandino, Shakti Gawain, Prince, Marc Allen, Lenedra J. Carroll, Anthony Robbins, Deepak Chopra, Paul Ferrini, Faye Mandell, Brock Tully, Helen Schucman & William Thetford, Gary Zukav, Herman Hesse, Joe Vitale, Jack Canfield, Tom Johnson, Barbara Sher, Pat O'Bryan, **and Most Importantly You.**

INTRODUCTION

It Wants You, Too

I saw a marvelous billboard advertising the sleek BMW Z-4 sports car. The ad simply splashed a photo of the shiny car and proclaimed, "It wants you, too."

The sign was teaching a crucial metaphysical lesson: The good you seek is seeking you. If you deeply desire a mate with certain characteristics, someone just like that is looking for someone like you. If you have a house to sell, someone is in the market for a house like yours. If you need a job, an employer needs someone with your unique skills.

The universe functions in perfect balance. The voice of fear and lack tells you that you are small, alone, and abandoned, and you have to struggle to get what you want and need. The voice of trust and abundance reminds you that all is well, you do not walk alone, and you are provided for in a million ways you do not understand and cannot manipulate. Fortunately, the voice of trust is far closer to the truth than the voice of fear, so you do not need to pay a moment's attention to the ranting of desperation. You are not desperate, so don't act like you are.

In a talk I recently gave in a church, I mentioned one of my favorite films, *Standing in the Shadows of Motown*, a documentary about a little-known group of musicians behind nearly all of the great Motown hits. After the service, a fellow came up to me and told me, "My brother produced that movie. Before the story was a movie, it was a book. Author Allan Slutsky searched for years for a movie producer, to no apparent avail. Then one day he was sitting next to a fellow on an airplane and he told his seat mate about his dream to turn the book into a movie. My brother liked the idea and produced it."

You have no idea how or when a dream might come true. If you want your dream to come true, you have to be true to it. Then let the great Law of Attraction help you with the details. It wants you, too.

Barry's book, well - **It wants you, too.**

You hold in your hands a simple and profound guide to Consciously Creating Your Own Life. Barry chose to understand this concept deeply, and he chooses to share it with others. He calls this powerful ability we use each and every moment - **The Creation Vibration**.

I have truly benefitted from Barry's wisdom. I know you will too. In fact, nothing would make me happier than knowing that Barry's book helped you access more joy in your life. Because it is from your place of Joy, that your Creation Vibration Attracts each and every dream, every job, every relationship, you want. It wants you, too.

---- **Alan Cohen**
Author of *Relax into Wealth*, *A Deep Breath of Life*,
Why Your Life Sucks,* and *Linden's Last Life
www.alancohen.com

TO THE READER

If you are reading this book Right Now, I Imagine it is because you wish to Consciously Create your Experience and more importantly the life of your Dreams, without limits and without compromise.

The tools you can use to clearly understand, define, and Create your Experience and your Dreams are presented here for you to use when you are ready. Let me just say, You are ready! Start today!

All of your life is orchestrated by your thoughts, feelings, words, and actions to deny or Create the life of your dreams exactly as you Choose to deny or Create your life through your very own thoughts, feelings, words, and actions.

There are over one million words in the English language. The average number of words used by any person is 5,000. Doctors use 5,000 Doctor words. Successful people use 5,000 Successful words. You use 5,000 words specific to your experience. I use 5,000 words specific to my experience.

What 5,000 words do you use to define and Create your Experience? If you are uncertain, you need only look at your Current life Experience because it is a result of your thoughts, feelings, words, and actions in motion. If you wish new experiences, Choose 5,000 new words.

Our words reach into the Un-Manifested Pure Potential of God/Life/Energy and Manifest the Intent within our words as our reality. Whatever we think, feel, and say is real becomes our reality.

On any given day, we may use as few as 100 words to set our Creative Intent in motion. On a bad day, we may use only 100 words that deny our Joy and Potential. On a good day, we may use only 100 words that Encourage our Joy and Potential. Our Words have the power to destroy or Create in OUR OWN Experience.

I AM Creating MY OWN Experience. I stress the idea, MY OWN because many problems in my past were a result of trying to Create someone else's Experience.

I AM Creating MY OWN Experience. You are Creating YOUR OWN Experience. If I were Creating YOUR OWN Experience, you would do everything I wanted. You would talk the way I talk, think the way I think, feel the way I feel, and do the things I do. We know that is impossible, although most of us have thought, at one time or another, that we had little control in our life.

I wrote this book as an instruction manual so that I could define the simple systems I use to Consciously Create MY OWN Experience and to Consciously Connect with God to Experience more Joy and Potential in my life.

You have Created this book to be in your life Right Now to benefit your Creative Abilities Immensely, Wonderfully, Completely, and Consciously.

Choose to Consciously Create Your Experience
Barry Thomas Bechta

I Consciously Bless All People, Places, and
Things in my experience with my
Love, Success, Abundance,
Peace, Health,
and Joy

RIGHT HERE RIGHT NOW

Right Now Is The Only Moment Of Creation

Right Now is the beginning of everything I shall ever Create, **Right Now**. Once this moment passes, its Creative Intent will have been placed into motion by me.

Every moment is a new beginning, a new Point of Creation. **Right Now** is another Point of Creation. **Right Now** is a second Point of Creation. Every single Moment, every single **Right Now** is another Point of Creation.

In the beginning (**Right Now**) there is God (or not) by my Choices and my Choices alone. Only I can make my Choices.

God is Absolutely All That Is. There is nothing that is not God. God is every person, place, thing, and experience. No matter what appears to be, God is All Of It. God is the Source of All That Is. This Source is Eternal and Everlasting. This Source is Pure Potential. I Access, Activate, and Attract the Manifestation of this Pure Potential through my thoughts and feelings.

God/Life/Energy is the Pure Potential. I AM Creating My Own Experience

GOD IS ENERGY

The Pure Potential Of God Is Pure Energy

Everything is formed from The Energy of God.

Rocks, Plants, Stars, People, Thoughts, and Feelings are all composed from The Energy of God. The Energy of God moves at different rates of Vibration.

At a microscopic level, everything is made up of moving particles. Even a rock, which appears to be solid and motionless on the surface, is actually full of moving Energy. The Speed at which Energy moves is called Vibration.

Every Person, Place, Thing, and Experience is composed of Vibrating Energy. Each Vibration is specific to a particular Manifestation in Physical Form. Everything has a Vibrational Core Signature in our Vibrational Universe.

A Star's Vibration Manifests as a Star
A Rock's Vibration Manifests as a Rock
A Plant's Vibration Manifests as a Plant
A Person's Vibration Manifests as a Person
A Thought's Vibration Manifests as a Thought
A Feeling's Vibration Manifests as a Feeling

VIBRATIONAL UNIVERSE

I Live In A Vibrational Universe

In every moment (**Right Now**) a particular Vibration emanates from me. All of my thoughts, feelings, words, and actions Vibrate at a particular Frequency in my experience. My Choices Attract people, places, things, and experiences that match my Vibrational Frequency.

Whatever feelings I experience, my energy Vibrates at a matching Frequency. My Vibrational Frequency Attracts people, places, things, and experiences that match whatever Vibrational Frequency I Access and Activate. If I feel something, I AM Accessing and Activating that Vibrational Frequency.

My thoughts Vibrate at a particular Frequency as well. My thoughts may be expressed as my words or as my actions. All of my thoughts, words, and actions Access and Activate whatever Vibrational Frequencies I Choose. Whenever I think, speak, or act upon something I AM Accessing and Activating that Vibrational Frequency.

My Creation Vibration matches my feeling Vibrations as I define them.

My bad feelings Attract bad feeling Creations.

My Good Feelings Attract Good feeling Creations.

MY CREATION VIBRATION

My Vibrational Frequency Attracts Unto Itself

The Law of Attraction is very simple. I Choose whatever I experience in my life through my thoughts, feelings, words, and actions.

If I am unsure about what I AM Attracting into my life, I need only look at my experiences to see what I have Attracted. If I Feel hole and incomplete, that is what my Creation Vibration Attracts. If I Feel Whole and Complete in my life experience, that is what my Creation Vibration Attracts. My Creation Vibration Attracts matching Vibrational Experiences to me.

Hole and incomplete feelings within me set my Creation Vibration to Attract people, places, things, and experiences that Allow me to experience my hole and incomplete Vibrational Core.

Whole and Complete feelings within me set my Creation Vibration to Attract people, places, things, and experiences that Allow me to experience my Whole and Complete Vibrational Core.

THE LAW OF ATTRACTION

My Creation Vibration Attracts My Experiences

My current life experiences are a result of my current Creation Vibration. My current Creation Vibration is a result of my thoughts, feelings, words, and actions.

Since my thoughts and my feelings inform my words and actions, for the rest of this book I shall talk about thoughts and feelings as being the basis of my Core Intentions and my Creation Vibration.

If I have the same old experiences, then I am also continuing to use my same old thoughts and feelings.

If I desire to have new and different experiences, then all I have to do is Consciously Choose new and different thoughts and feelings.

My thoughts and feelings are the process through which I Create my Own Experience. I Choose my thoughts and feelings, and my experiences are Attracted to me. I Can Choose my thoughts and feelings unconsciously or Consciously. It is always and only my Choice to make.

I AM CREATING MY OWN EXPERIENCE

I AM Creating My Own Experience

Always in all ways, I Create my own experience through my thoughts and feelings. My thoughts and feelings Attract people, places, things, and experiences which match my Creation Vibration.

My Happy thoughts and feelings Create my Vibrations of Happiness and Attract people, places, things, and experiences of Happiness.

My Bored thoughts and feelings Create my Vibrations of Boredom and Attract people, places, things, and experiences of Boredom.

My Angry thoughts and feelings Create my Vibrations of Anger and Attract people, places, things, and experiences of Anger.

My Confused thoughts and feelings Create my Vibrations of Confusion and Attract people, places, things, and experiences of Confusion.

Whatever thoughts and feelings I have Create my Vibrations of Whatever I focus upon and Attract people, places, things, and experiences of Whatever I energize.

I CHOOSE EVERYTHING I EXPERIENCE

I Choose Absolutely Everything I Experience

When I think about the things I enjoy in my experience, the concept that I Choose everything is easier to understand.

However, the idea that I Choose Absolutely Everything in my experience is hard to understand when I think about the people, places, and things that I wished were not in my experience, **(I shall talk more about this very soon)**.

My thoughts and feelings Create my Vibrations which Attract my Experiences. Through my life I have used many thoughts and feelings to Create many Vibrations to Attract many Experiences sometimes unconsciously and other times Consciously.

For example, when I Consciously decide I would love to learn some new computer skills. My decision is a new thought that sets my Creation Vibration which Attracts my Experiences. All of a sudden my new thoughts and feelings put me in touch with information about computer courses, people who love computers, and many other computer experiences. My computer thoughts Create my computer Vibrations which Attract my computer related experiences.

MY CREATION VIBRATION CORE CONCEPT

My Creation Vibration Always Attracts My Experiences

I AM The DJ (Disc Jockey) of my life. My thoughts and feelings Create Vibrations which Attract people whom like to sing and dance to the same tunes I do, while at the same time repelling all people whom like to sing and dance to different tunes.

If I like the tune I AM singing and dancing to, I need only keep Choosing it and playing it. When I AM ready for something else, I can Choose a different tune.

In my past, I sung the story of my life. My life story was presented primarily in two different songs:

WOE IS ME   or   **WOW IS ME**

UNCONSCIOUS OR CONSCIOUS CORE

My Core Concept Can Be Unconscious Or Conscious

My thoughts and feelings used one time have very little effect on my experience. My habitual thoughts and feelings unconsciously set my Core Intention unless I Consciously Choose my Intention **Right Now**.

My Core Intention defines me as the person I AM. In each and every moment I Choose my Core Intention by default or by Decision.

My thoughts and feelings (Core Intention) Create my Vibrations which Attract my Experiences.

 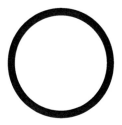

unconscious Core   Conscious Core
many thoughts and feelings   One Thought/Feeling

ONE OR MANY INTENTIONS

My Core Intention Creates Powerfully With One Intent

In every moment **Right Now** I either rely unconsciously on all of my past thoughts and feelings to set my Core Intention, or I Consciously Choose my Core Intention **Right Now**.

When I rely on all of my past thoughts and feelings as my Core Intention, then all of my habitual Choices and preferences make up my Core Intention. All of my deepest heartfelt most secret beliefs Create my Vibrations which Attract my Experiences.

Thoughts or feelings that I activate a few times rarely become my Core Intention. Thoughts and feelings I habitually Choose as my preferences become my Core Intention.

I like ice cream.
I don't like Mondays.
Why do I only have just enough?
I'm lucky in love.
I'm unlucky with money.
Why don't they understand?
Love actually is all around.

EMOTIONALLY GUIDED OPINIONS

My Habitual Thoughts And Feelings Form My Intentions

My ego (emotionally guided opinions) speaks in my life about things I MUST be, do, or have because I win with them or I lose without them.

My ego uses thoughts and feelings that encourage fear, worry, desperation, anger, frustration, grief, guilt, revenge, jealousy, powerlessness, impatience, pessimism, hatred, doubt, boredom, blame, confusion, depression, and incompleteness.

My ego speaks in emotionally guided opinions of what can go wrong, how badly I am going to feel, and the total worthlessness of my Choices.

When I Habitually Choose my ego as my guide in life, my life is guided to ever increasing levels of feeling worse about myself, others, and the potential in all life.

Only I can Choose my thoughts and feelings. Others can share their thoughts and feelings with me. Only I can Choose my thoughts and feelings. I can Choose the emotionally guided opinions of my ego or I can Choose God Giving Ongoing Direction in my life. It is my Choice.

GIVING ONGOING DIRECTION

God Gives Ongoing Direction To Joy

The Voice of God Giving Ongoing Direction in my life speaks about experiences I can Be, Do, or Have just for the Fun of them.

The Voice of God within me uses thoughts and feelings that encourage Passion, Possibilities, Optimism, Hopefulness, Joy, Contentment, Belief, Eagerness, Love, Freedom, Potential, Success, Abundance, Peace, Health, Appreciation, Enthusiasm, Encouragement, Blessings, and Completeness.

The Voice of God Giving Ongoing Direction in my life speaks of what can go Right, how Joyous I AM going to feel, and the total Worthiness of my Choices.

When I Habitually Choose God as my guide in life, my life is guided to ever increasing levels of feeling Better about myself, others, and the potential in all life.

Joy as my guiding Compass works whether I rely on my unconscious Core Intentions or Choose my Conscious Core Intentions. God Giving Ongoing Direction in my life, waits for me to place my Intention into motion, through my thoughts, feelings, words, and actions, and then gives me guidance in response to my Intentions.

JOY IS MY COMPASS

. . . God Is Joy Is God Is Joy Is God . . .

Absolutely every thought and feeling I use in a day (and there are thousands and thousands I use in a given day), combine to form my Core Intention, unless and until I specify my Core Intention in the moment **Right Now**.

The great confusion of being the Creator of my own Experience is that in my past, I unconsciously Choose my habitual thoughts and feelings as my Core Intention. When the Creations that resulted in my life were far from my desires I could not understand the way in which I had Chosen what was in my experience.

Right Now using Joy as my Compass, I can Consciously Choose my Core Intention. My Core Intention Creates a Vibration which Attracts my Experiences. The process of Creating my Own Experience Consciously and Constantly Accesses, Activates, and Attracts Joy in three specific ways:

Intend Joy
Feel Joy
Choose Joy

INTEND JOY, FEEL JOY, CHOOSE JOY

My Thoughts And Feelings Intend, Feel, And Choose Joy

Right Now all of my thoughts and feelings are intending, feeling, and Choosing my Experience; whether I know it or not; whether I AM Conscious of this process or not. When I Choose to Consciously take Responsibility of my Creative Power through my Choices, my life changes dramatically. Only I can make the Choice to Consciously Choose my Experience of Joy.

thoughts and feelings
that depress and deny
Joy and Potential

thoughts and feelings
that Uplift and Encourage
Joy and Potential

I INTEND JOY RIGHT NOW

I Choose My Experience By My Thoughts And Feelings

Right Now all of my thoughts and feelings are attracting my level of Joy. Whatever my Experience is **Right Now** is a result of my thoughts and feelings. When I look at my habitual thoughts and feelings I see that my Core Intention Attracts as much Joy as possible or not. Examples of my past thoughts have included:

I love my Job. I hate my Job. **She rubs me the right way.** He rubs me the wrong way. **What a beautiful day.** Of all the days it could rain. **I love that coat.** Just give me a few damn minutes. **Your hair looks fantastic.** This never goes on sale. **I found $20 on the ground today.** Leave your brother alone. **This past weekend was the best of my life.** Shut up! **Love you.** Lazy SOB. **Thank you.** I'll never get out of this job. **I Define my dreams because I create them.** How the hell did I create this? **You're doing a fabulous job.** I'm so confused. **I AM on a roll.** You said you were going to do it! **God Blesses us all.** Where is God in all of this? **I love making joyful passionate love with you.** Leave me alone! **I Love having more than enough for Right Now.** Life Sucks! **Life is set up for everyone to win.**

I FEEL JOY RIGHT NOW

I Consciously Choose My Thoughts And Feelings

My purpose and place in life is unique. No other person has the exact makeup that I have. My purpose in life is a combination of all my preferences about life.

All of my thoughts and feelings inform and build all of my preferences: my livelihood preferences, my relationship preferences, my sexual preferences, my love preferences, my living accommodation preferences, my friend preferences, my Joy preferences, and in fact my preferences for absolutely everything in my life.

Whether I Choose my Core Intention Consciously or unconsciously, God Gives Ongoing Direction in my life though my feelings of Joy. When I Choose thoughts and feelings that Uplift and Encourage Joy and Potential, they make up my Core Intention that Vibrates and Attracts more of the same.

Most Importantly when I Consciously Choose all of my thoughts and feelings to Uplift and Encourage Joy and Potential in my life, I Powerfully Ask for, Align with, Allow, and Accept God's Joy and Potential as my life Experience.

I CHOOSE JOY RIGHT NOW

When I Feel Joy, I AM Attracting My Dreams Effortlessly

In the human experience feeling Joy is sometimes the first experience, but not always. Nonetheless in the process of Consciously Intending, Feeling, and Choosing Joy, it becomes much easier to experience Joy first and foremost.

> **Intend Joy:** My Intentions are made up of my thoughts and feelings. I Consciously Intend Joy in every moment of Creation **Right Now**.

> **Feel Joy:** When I feel Joy I know I AM Aligned with my Core Intentions within God. Joy is my Compass **Right Now.**

> **Choose Joy:** When anything challenges my sense of Joy, I need only Choose a single thought that Uplifts and Encourages Joy and Potential in my life **Right Now.**

THE GIFT WITHIN ALL EXPERIENCES

One Joyful Uplifting Thought Attracts My Joy Right Now

The gift within all experiences is the same gift. The gift within all experiences is my ability to Choose my Connection to God. My Connection to God is active when I experience a feeling of Joy in my life.

Even in the darkest of experiences I can Choose to Connect with my feeling of Joy. One simple Uplifting thought Connects me with Joy in my life. My one Uplifting thought Attracts more Joy to me and adds more Joy to the sum total of Joy in the Universe.

The gift in every experience is not something I find outside of me. The gift is a Choice I make within me. When I Choose an Uplifting thought, I Vibrate with an Uplifting Vibration and I Attract Uplifting Experiences.

Whatever person, place, thing, or experience I encounter in life, there is always a gift that I can Access and Activate and Attract into my life by my Choice and my Choice alone. When I Intend, Choose, and Feel Joy, I Vibrate and Attract Joy into my life.

All of my Joyful thoughts Attract more of the same Vibrational Experiences. My Creation Vibration is set to Joy.

ALL OF MY FEELINGS ATTEMPT TO UPLIFT ME

My Feelings Attract More Of The Same Feelings

All of my feelings Attract more of the same Vibrational Experiences. Every feeling I feel can Uplift me from some other feeling I feel.

Feelings like anger, jealousy, frustration, impatience, and revenge depress and deny my Ultimate Joy and Potential, yet they can Access and Activate a feeling that is better than some previous feeling I had.

Anger Uplifts me from powerlessness.
Jealousy Uplifts me from despair.
Frustration Uplifts me from depression.
Impatience Uplifts me from guilt.
Revenge Uplifts me from blame.

Feelings that depress and deny my Ultimate Joy and Potential are unproductive only when I Choose them continually. When I Choose a feeling like anger to Uplift me from a feeling like powerlessness, and then Choose a different feeling to Uplift me from anger I move closer towards my Ultimate Joy and Potential. All feelings can ultimately benefit my Journey and my Oneness with God.

THE IMPORTANCE OF MY FEELINGS

I AM My Feelings Not My Forms

When my physical form dies, my spirit lives on. When my spirit lives on, I take all of the thoughts and feelings I experienced in my life with me. My spirit does not take any physical forms with it. My spirit is only a collection of all my thoughts and feelings.

I AM a collection of thoughts and feelings, instead of my physical form. I AM a collection of thoughts and feelings, rather than my material possessions. I AM my feelings instead of the forms of my life.

The following two questions bring up very different feeling answers pertaining to my experience:

1.   If I ***always*** get the forms I imagine in my life and ***never*** feel Joyful, how would I feel about my life?

2.   If I ***never*** get the forms I imagine in my life and I ***always*** feel Joyful, how would I feel about my life?

I DEFINE MY LIFE BECAUSE I CREATE IT

I Love Creating The Feelings And The Forms I Desire

My thoughts and feelings define my life. My thoughts and feelings Create Vibrations which Attract my Experiences. Through practice the process of Conscious Creation becomes simpler and more understandable.

When my thoughts and feelings Ask for, Align with, Allow, and Accept my most Loving, Successful, Abundant, Peaceful, Healthy, Joyful, and Miraculous ideas which Attract my Experiences, I also Ask for, Align with, Allow, and Accept God's Joyous Vision for my life.

God is Energy. The Energy of God is Pure Potential. God is Every Possibility ever Imaginable. There is nothing God is not. God is the Source and Supply of All That Is. God is Always in All Ways Joy and Potential.

A belief in God is not essential for these concepts to work. People who do not believe in God still use these Concepts to Create their life experiences.

My belief in God only enhances my Connection to all my Experiences. My belief in God Allows me to Access the Energy that makes up God/Life/Energy. My belief in God reminds me that All of life is One, all people are connected, and that We Are All One.

I CONSCIOUSLY CREATE MY EXPERIENCES

All Of My Life Experiences Are A Result Of My Choices

I Accept that everything has a purpose in my life. The purpose of everything is to remind me that I Choose Absolutely Everything in my life. Conscious Creation is my Complete Connection with All That Is in my life.

When I feel connected with All That Is, my life flows easily and effortlessly. This easy and effortless flow is a result of being totally Conscious of my Creations.

I Accept Complete Responsibility for my Creative thoughts and feelings. I Accept Complete Responsibility for everything I Experience in my life. I Can only Accept my Creative Choices in my Experiences.

The Creative Choices and experiences of other people are their Responsibility. I Can Only Create and Perceive my own Experience. I Consciously Create my Experience by Intending Joy, Feeling Joy, and Choosing Joy.

Absolutely Everything in my experience is there through my Choices. Now that I know the process of Conscious Creation in my life, I Consciously Choose it.

ONE CERTAINTY OR LIMITLESS POTENTIAL

Whatever Is In My Core Ripples Into My Life Experiences

The repetitive nature of life and the repetitive nature of this book are purposely designed to remind me that I Create everything I think and feel **Repeatedly**.

My thoughts and feelings Manifest into my experiences. My unconscious thoughts and feelings Create unconscious and unexpected forms. My Conscious thoughts and feelings Create Conscious and expected forms.

Unless and until I Consciously Choose my Core Intention at the deepest heartfelt most secret parts of my being, unintentional Vibrational experiences appear to show up. I Consciously Choose my Creation Vibration.

Part of the confusion about Conscious Creation occurs when I Consciously set my Creation Vibration **Right Now**. For example, I Consciously Intend the acquisition of a particular automobile. My thoughts and feelings about this one particular automobile Create my Vibrations for that one particular automobile which Attracts my experiences of that one particular automobile. This One Certainty pushes away the Limitless Potential of all other possible automobiles.

PREFERENCES AND EXPECTATIONS

My Core Intention Is One Certainty Or Limitless Potential

Whether my Core Intention involves a sports car, a job, a home, or a relationship, I can set my preference to be one and the same. My One Certainty is that the Limitless Potential of God Manifests All That Is in my life.

I define who I Choose to be through the things I prefer. All of my thoughts and feelings automatically define my preferences.

I define what I would prefer to be, do, have, or experience in my life, and then I Ask for, Align with, Allow, and Accept God's Version of my Visions.

Within all of my Conscious Creations, I prefer a particular feeling within the forms of my Experience. When the feelings are present, even though the forms maybe different, rarely do I care. When I careless about the forms and I live in Positive Expectation, I feel a sense of Joy with all Creations as I anticipate my preferred Creations.

However when the forms matter MOST to me, I live in a state of negative expectation, where my emotionally guided opinions rule my experience.

IMAGINATION AND MEDITATION

Positive Expectation Is My Preferred State Of Joy

When I pray for particular forms, I AM really seeking the feelings within those forms. When I focus on the feelings and careless about the forms, the forms I dream about come to me effortlessly.

All of my thoughts and feelings constantly ask God for the things I desire. God knows what I dream about. When I make Joy my prime focus in life, God takes care of the forms in my life to fulfil my Joyful Experiences.

Controlling my thoughts and feelings Consciously speeds up the process of Manifestation in my life. God knows what I dream about because God knows what I consistently think and feel. Sometimes my thoughts and feelings even work towards attracting the things I dream about.

Two powerful tools I use to focus upon and intensify my feelings are my Imagination and Meditation. When I Imagine something, I intensify the feelings I associate with particular forms in my experience.

When I Meditate, I think about nothing and just Allow the feelings of God's Joy into my Heart, Mind, and Being.

GOD LOVES ME

God Loves Me For My Joyousness Tells Me So

God is All of Life. Absolutely every person, place, thing, and experience in my life is God. God Supports and Loves all my choices through Free Will.

I can Choose Heaven or hell and like a photocopier, God reproduces whatever I Choose.

Hell is my inability to control or change or love whatever is Now Here.

Heaven is my ability to Allow and Accept and Love whatever is Now Here.

God reproduces whatever I Choose:
whether I like it or not.
whether I AM Conscious or not.
whether I want it or not.
whether I Choose Heaven or not.

I Intend to Choose things that make me feel Loved, Abundant, Successful, Peaceful, Joyful, Healthy, Cared for, and Miraculous in every moment and especially when things appear challenging.

I LOVE MYSELF FULLY

I Love That God Faithfully Reproduces What I Choose

I Love myself fully. I Love others and God fully; All of Life; every person, place, thing, and experience. I Love my mistakes and my habits and my dreams.

I can only Change the things I Love about myself. I Can only Change myself. When I Love myself fully, I allow people to be who they are because my Love comes from a feeling inside of me.

When I Love myself fully, I respect that other people may wish to do different things from me. I respect the space of others and they respect my space. If I Choose to enter the space of others in ways that make them feel uncomfortable, other people generally enter my space in ways that make me feel uncomfortable.

In my past, whenever I felt a need to criticize others, or make fun of others, or help others, or to do whatever others were doing in order to be a part of the group, I also desperately needed to feel love inside myself.

Right Now, When I love myself fully, I love others fully as they are showing up and it is easy for me to Love and Bless them because of the person I AM.

ONE MONTH TO NEW HABITS

I Bless Life Through All Of My Thoughts And Feelings

It takes at least one month of making a Choice consistently to form a new habit. It can take more than one month to reprogram a deeply rooted habit by making a different choice consistently. My new habits Create my new Experiences.

In my past, I used the garbage in, garbage out habit system. The garbage in(side of me) became the garbage out(side of me).

My current life experiences come from my current habits. If I keep my current thought and feeling habits, I shall also keep creating the same thought and feeling experiences. I understand and accept that some (and sometimes many) of my experiences have felt painful through my current thought and feeling habits.

Now I let go and I let God. To let go of my old habits it takes at least one month of consistent work Choosing a new habit. To let God, I Choose new habits that Ask for, Align with, Allow, and Accept God's Manifestation of my dreams. When I Ask for, Align with, Allow, and Accept where I desire to be over where I believe I am, then I experience my dreams in physical form.

THANK YOU EGO FOR MY
EMOTIONALLY GUIDED OPINIONS

I Love And Bless My Emotionally Guided Opinions

Ego, I Bless you and Thank you and Love you as I Release you and Accept God Giving Ongoing Direction in this very moment which suggests I can Choose beliefs and habits that promote and support the most Loving, Successful, Abundant, Peaceful, Joyous, Healthy, and Miraculous Experiences Right Here Right Now.

Mistakes are only habits that take me in a direction away from where I desire to be. I make mistakes as I Create new habits, until I AM One with God in my life.

I get out of my ego mind and release all my emotionally guided opinions about what is Now Here in relation to what came before.

Without opinions and Only my Intention for Joy, I Ask for, Align with, Allow, and Accept the Joy of God Available Right Here Right Now.

My ego mind communicates with thoughts and feelings that deny my Joy and Potential. My ego mind is full of questions and thinks in limits.

God in my Heart communicates with thoughts and feelings that Attract my Joy and Potential. God in my Heart is full of Answers and Thanks and Loves it.

GOD IS MY POWER

God Is The Only Power Within My Life

God is the Power within everything. God does everything without the most powerful people in the world. When a powerful person dies, the world is still here.

Everything in my life is attracted to me by what I believe about myself at the very deepest part of my being. I Intend to Ask for, Align with, Allow, and Accept God as the Power in my life.

I become Powerful when I become Power Smart. Power Smart people clean up their garbage in(side), which cleans up their garbage out(side).

I Choose to clean up my thoughts and feelings of Love and Worthiness with God in(side of me). I Choose to keep myself clean, my clothes clean, my room clean, and my house clean out(side of me) because my outer world mirrors the Love and Worthiness I hold about myself in my inner world.

I AM Power Smart with all my energy use when as much of God's Power expressed through me as possible is focussed upon and Attracting all of my dreams.

I AM CALM AND PEACEFULLY HEALTHY

My Calm And Peaceful Nature Is Healthy

I Create healthy habits through my Choices. For my body, I Choose to eat healthy and nourishing food, drink water galore, exercise regularly, brush and floss my teeth after every meal, and get plenty of sleep.

For my mind, I Choose to love all my thoughts, feelings, words, actions, and I Choose to Love every person, place, thing, and experience in my life. I can find at least one thing I Love about everything in my life.

I Choose to slow down and take all the time I need to see and feel God in every person, place, thing, and experience. I Intend to be calm, respectful, loving, honest, and trustworthy with myself and everyone.

For my spirit, I Choose to connect with God as much as possible each and every moment of my life. When I think about God, I Connect with God. The more I think about God in Loving ways, the more effectively I Connect with God and All of Life in Loving Ways.

When I Connect with my Joy and Potential, I feel Joyous and Uplifted by my Connection to All That Is (God) and All That Is (Good). The Feeling of God is The Feeling of Good.

I AM RESPONSIBLE THROUGH MY JOY

I AM Joyfully Responsible

I AM the only one responsible for my life. I AM Only Responsible for me. I AM the only one who can Choose my habits. I AM the only one who can Change my habits. I Choose everything I think, feel, say, and do.

I Choose to release my disappointments, anger, and frustrations without hurting myself or others. I Choose to be Joyful over being right. I Choose to help myself and others be Joyful in respectful ways.

I use appropriate humour that Allows everyone to feel Joyful and comfortable. The way I can tell that everyone is genuinely Joyful is to notice how other people are acting and reacting with me. Joy bubbles effortlessly in my life.

When someone is not Joyful, I AM Aware of their disconnection, yet I focus on my Connection to Joy. When I feel Joy, I AM Connected with my Joy and Share it easily. When I AM Responsible I have the ability to respond appropriately with All of Life. My Joy Connects me to the Win-Win Potential available to everyone Always in All Ways.

I INTEND GOD

I Consciously Intend God In My Life

God provides everything in life. I rarely get the things I desire when I pursue them. I always get the things I desire when I Attract them. The only way to Attract something into my life is by Consciously Choosing and Controlling my Attention within my inner world.

My thoughts and feelings make up my inner world. Only I Can Choose and Control my thoughts and feelings. It is my Responsibility and no one else's.

I Intend to Change my world experience from garbage in(side) garbage out(side) to God In(side) God Out(side). I Foster and Create this Change by Consciously Choosing my beliefs and habits of God until they become my unconscious and automatic beliefs and habits.

I Intend to deeply Love, Trust, Respect, and be Honest with myself and God (Absolutely everything in life). Every person, place, thing, and experience in my life is God. All Is God/Life/Energy.

I Intend God. I Intend Good. I Intend Greatness. I Intend Joy. I Intend Potential. I Intend Love. I Intend Blessings.

I INTEND GOD 100%

All Of My Thoughts And Feelings Are My Intentions

I Intend God 100%. Intending 100% is like being pregnant. When it comes to being pregnant, there is no 50% pregnant. A woman is either pregnant (100%) or not pregnant (0%).

Life provides whatever I Intend. Either I Intend (100%) or I do not intend (0%). Wherever I place my Attention, I also place my Intention in my experience.

When I place my Attention on 1% fear, doubt, or worry, I AM intending fear, doubt, or worry 100% in that moment. Similarly, when I place my Attention on 1% Love, Faith, Certainty, I AM Intending Love, Faith, Certainty 100% in that moment.

In my life, I can Intend my Connection with God 100% or I can Intend disconnection. It is my Choice and my Choice alone.

When I focus upon challenging experiences in my life, I deny my Joy and I AM out of Alignment with God and my purpose in life.

When I focus upon Amazing Experiences, I feel Joy and I Align with God and my purpose in life.

I THANK GOD

I Thank God For Absolutely Everything In My Life

Everyday I take the time to Consciously Connect with God. I breathe in deeply, and I breathe in the Love of God deeply while Creating a Vibration of God through the Creation Vibration words (UM) and (AH)

I take the time to meditate in this fashion as often during the day as possible to totally Activate my Connection with God in my life. I can Choose to feel disconnected or I can Choose to feel Connected. It is a Choice only I can make.

I Intend to Choose Habits of Feeling Connected with God Always in All Ways.

Thank You God for our Powerful Connection and for Your Power Providing everything in my Life. With You God, I have the most Loving, Successful, Abundant, Peaceful, Healthy, Joyous, and Miraculous Habits Right Here Right Now.

Thank You God for Absolutely every person, place, thing, and experience in my life, which reminds me that I Can Choose You God Always in All Ways.

I JOYOUSLY DO WHAT I LOVE

My Joyous Thoughts Lead To My Joy

Love Hour: Each day I take some time just for myself. When I focus on the things that I love, my Joyous feelings set my Creation Vibration. My Joyous Creation Vibration Attracts my experiences of Joy. One Hour is a very small commitment to Create the life of my dreams. Only I can make the time for my Joy and my Dreams. If I devote one love hour each day to my dreams for an entire year, that equals 365 hours (or nine - forty hour weeks plus five additional hours). When I work in a dream livelihood just over nine weeks, I can accomplish amazing things. I start today.

10% Solution: On my journey to Create my new habits and experiences I use the 10% Solution. When I make a commitment to Joyously direct 10% of my time, energy, and resources towards my dreams, I Attract people, places, things, and experiences that build my dreams. For example, with the *Love Hour* concept I can start with 10% of that hour, or 6 minutes to begin fostering my Joy and my dreams. The *10% Solution* means that I Consciously Choose thoughts, feelings, words, and actions which consistently Uplift and Encourage my Joy and Potential. I Choose my thoughts and feelings, God Manifests them. My Ultimate Connection with God Always in All Ways results by taking Simple steps regularly.

I LET MY LIFE FLOW

My Choices Create My Dreams

I do what I love and the money follows: When I follow my dreams and desires I feel Joy. When I AM Conscious that my Joy Attracts and Allows my dreams and desires to Manifest effortlessly, my life flows easily and I do the things I enjoy. I make Choices that Uplift and Encourage others and myself. My Confidence and Connection to Joy and God Manifests everything in my life. I do what I love and the Abundance I require to live my dreams and desires Manifests Joyously.

I let it go and it comes to me: When I focus on Joy in life, everything I could ever Imagine comes to me. When my thoughts and feelings focus Only upon that which I desire, my desires Manifest automatically. I let go of my emotionally guided opinions and my Joy bubbles easily. I release my expectations and my preferences come to me. I Choose everything in my life that repels from me and everything that comes to me. I Choose everything by my unconscious decisions or my Conscious Choices. My life Experience is always a result of my Choices.

WHATEVER I GIVE I LIVE

My Thoughts And Feelings Give Me life

Whatever I Give my Attention to, I Live in my Experience. I Live what I Give to life **Right Now** and my Creation Vibration Attracts more of the same for me to Experience.

Feeling hole and incomplete: When my Core Intention is a feeling of being incomplete, my inner hole subtracts and swallows up everything in my life that is hole and incomplete. Negative feelings are of great value when I AM Able to use them to quickly remind me that my energy use is denying my dreams and desires.

Feeling Whole and Complete: When my Core Intention is a feeling of being Complete, my inner Wholeness Attracts and Allows everything in my life that is Whole and Complete. Positive feelings remind me that my energy use is Creating my dreams and desires.

I Give whatever I Live: All of my thoughts and feelings Attract my experiences. As a result, everything I experience, I give to myself. I Give whatever I Live, whether I want it or not. I Choose Consciously. I Intend Joy. I Feel Joy. I Choose Joy. I AM Joyful.

I AM CREATING MY OWN ANSWERS

God Gives Ongoing Direction Through My Feelings

With every decision in my life, my feelings are my guide. Whatever decision I need to make, my feelings tell me the way to proceed.

When I feel Joy, my answer is YES.
When I feel doubt, I wait it out
When I feel anger, my answer is no.
When I feel confused, I wait for Joy.
When I feel sad, I wait until I AM Glad.
When I feel anxious, I wait for relaxation.
When I feel unclear, I wait for clear feelings.
Any feeling other than Joy, means I wait.
I make effective decisions when I feel Joyful.

When I feel anything other than Joyful, I wait until I feel Joyful. To activate my Joyous feelings I Consciously Choose thoughts that Uplift and Encourage my Joy and Potential. One Joyous thought leads to other Joyous thoughts and to my feelings of Joy. It is always my Choice.

All of my answers are obvious when I feel Joyful

I AM CREATING MY OWN DREAMS

My Dreams Are God's Inspiration Through Me

My dreams and desires are energized by Joyful feelings. All of my dreams and desires are given to me by God. My dreams and desires are different from the dreams and desires of everyone else. My dreams and desires are there for me to Activate, Access, and Allow.

My dreams and desires are assured with God. God Provides everything in life I shall ever need to attain my dreams and desires. No matter what appears to be, my dreams are coming to fruition when I place my thoughts only on my dreams and follow my feelings of Joy.

My dreams and desires add my unique perspective to the fullness of God/Life/Energy. Everyone else's dreams and desires do the same. I need only focus on my own dreams and desires in order to Manifest them with God.

By the end of my current life experience on Earth, I shall accomplish the unique dreams and desires God and I have planned together. God provides all the people, place, things, resources, and experiences I require to Manifest my dreams and desires with God.

I AM CREATING MY OWN RELATIONSHIPS

I Create Every Relationship I Dream And Desire

My thoughts and feelings about All of my Relationships Creates my Vibrations that Attract my Relationship Experiences.

My Relationship Rings

My thoughts and feelings Always Attract all of my Relationships:

1. My Core
2. My Intimate
3. My Family
4. My Friends
5. My Community
6. My Country
7. My World

My Core Relationship with God, Vibrates and Attracts All of my other Relationship Rings to match my Core Beliefs. I Choose everyone in my experience.

I AM UNCONDITIONAL LOVE

I AM The Light In My World Experience

In today's society, most everyone can easily activate a negative world view. A world view that denies Joy and Potential in one's thoughts, feelings, words, actions, and experiences.

These same people require their life experiences to be a particular way before they can feel good. When they are unable to achieve their requirements, they resign themselves to unhappy and powerless lives. Just as easily, anyone may focus on anything they Choose in their experience.

Only I Can Choose my focus. I AM Free when I Choose what I desire and Allow others to do the same. I Attract people of like Vibration, and repel all others.

I Choose to be a light in the world. I Choose my thoughts and feelings to be Uplifting, Encouraging, and Healing. My Choice to Love others no matter what, Creates Who I AM. My Core Intention is to be Unconditionally Loving. My Expressions are Joyous. My ideas Encourage the dreams of others. The gift in every experience is my ability to share Unconditional Love through my Joyful thoughts, feelings, words, and actions.

I AM CREATING MY OWN ABUNDANCE

God Is My Abundance

With God as my Abundance, my Abundance is assured. The entire world is at my service. I need only place myself in Vibrational Harmony with any form of Abundance I desire and I Attract my experience of it.

I define my Abundance in Clear terms. I define the level of Lasting Financial Freedom I AM Creating. I define the ease and effortless nature of my Abundance. I define all of my life because I AM Creating My Own experience.

I know I AM in Vibrational Harmony with my Abundance when I feel Joyful. When I feel Joyful, my Creations come to me. I need only focus upon my Joyful thoughts and feelings about Abundance in order to Create my Abundance.

I have an Angel Accountant whom has secured for me an annual after tax income of over $1 Million. The way I receive the physical experience of this inheritance is by Joyfully spending (in my vibration) $2,739.73 each and every day. I keep a journal and I enjoy my Creation Vibrations knowing that they Attract my matching Vibrational experiences.

ABUNDANCE IS ALL THAT IS

I Create Abundance When I Contemplate Abundance

Whatever I focus upon, I Create. My thoughts and feelings Create my Vibrations about whatever I think and feel. When I think only about Abundance and feel Joyous, I Create Powerful Vibrations of Abundance which Attract my experiences of Abundance.

Abundance is All that Is. Life is Only Abundance. Even abundant lack is still an Abundance of lack. When I acknowledge and see Only Abundance with All of my thoughts and feelings, then Only Abundance Manifests in my life through me.

I cannot think of illness to Create Abundant Health.
I cannot think of my debts and Create Abundant Assets.
I cannot think of enemies to Create Loving Relationships.
I cannot think of any form of lack and Create Abundance.
I cannot think of limits and Create Limitless Abundance

My Joyful thoughts Create My Joyful Abundance
My thoughts of Abundance Create Abundance

I love having lots of abundance to . . .

I love having lots of money to . . .

I AM CREATING MY OWN SUCCESS

God's Joy Is My Right Livelihood

No matter what dreams and desires I have, God is Manifesting whatever I Ask for, Align with, Allow, and Accept into my experience through my Creation Vibration.

I Choose what I desire and dream as my ideal livelihood. God Provides All That I AM. My level of Joy indicates my Alignment with and Acceptance of God's Manifestation of my dreams and desires.

I only need to work Joyously and effortlessly towards my dreams and desires, while Consciously Intending Joy, Feeling Joy, and Choosing Joy in my life.

When I make Joy my Prime Purpose, my Right Livelihood and Success easily Manifests in even greater forms than I could ever have imagined.

I keep God's Joy employed in my life, and I replace the services of my emotionally guided opinions after they have alerted me to any negative focussed Creation.

I Keep God's Joy Employed

I AM CREATING MY OWN HAPPINESS

I Live My life For The Joy Of Life

Life, most importantly, is here for me to have fun. Joy is easily and always accessible through my thoughts. One thought can take me towards God's Joy and the Pure Potential available to me **Right Now**.

Everything is possible when I AM Connected with God in my life. My Connection is most readily apparent when I AM Happy and Joyful.

My ego (emotionally guided opinions) says I Must be, do, or have particular experiences because I win with them or I lose without them.

God Giving Ongoing Direction in my life says I can be, do, or have any experience Just for the Joy of it.

Creating my own experience is Fun when I Access the Joy of God available in each moment through my thoughts that Access, Activate, Attract, Align with, Allow, and Accept God's Joy. I Choose Joyously.

I AM RADIANT HEALTH AND BEAUTY

When I Live Joyously, I Live Healthfully

My Joy is Attracted by my
thoughts and feelings about my Joy.

My Abundance is Attracted by my
thoughts and feelings about my Abundance.

My Relationships are Attracted by my
thoughts and feelings about my Relationships.

My Right Livelihood is Attracted by my
thoughts and feelings about my Right Livelihood.

My Radiant Health and Beauty is Attracted by my
thoughts and feelings about my Radiant Health and Beauty.

Whatever I think and feel about my life is Created
as my life experience. I Consciously Create my Life.

This is the Principle of Creation:

My Contemplation of My World Creates My World.

THE LAW OF ATTRACTION IS CONSISTENT

My Contemplation Of My World Creates My World

The Law of Attraction is Constant and Consistent. Absolutely everything in my experience is a result of my thoughts and feelings.

When my thoughts and feelings match, they powerfully Create together. When my thoughts and feelings differ, my feelings become my prime Creation Activator.

My Good feelings Create more Good feelings. My Abundant feelings Create more Abundance. My Loving feelings Create more Love. Any feeling I activate, Vibrates as my Core Intention and ripples out into my experience and Attracts everything of like Vibrational Nature.

Only when I make a Conscious effort to Constantly and Consistently Intend Joy, Feel Joy, and Choose Joy do I understand how powerfully I AM Creating My Own Experience

All of my experiences are Chosen by me and me alone. Every person, place, and thing is brought to me by my thoughts and feelings. I have 100% Control. I Create it all.

GRATITUDE IS MY ATTITUDE

I Thank God For Everything I AM

I Thank God for everything in my life. God is the Source of everything. I Consciously Choose everything I desire to experience in my life, and God Provides everything, easily, effortlessly, and Joyously, no questions asked. I Thank God for everything I AM.

I Intended to write a Book that would Uplift myself and others. God Provided me with this very book. God Provided me with the words to write. I feel Joyous as I Create it. I feel Joyous as I Imagine you reading it.

Great ideas are life affirming in their simplicity. I have felt these simple concepts in my heart for most of my life. In my past, I unconsciously connected with them.

Right Now I Consciously Connect with them.

Right Now I Gratefully Connect with the simple concept of Joy as my Compass as I Redefine, Guide, and Inspire my Connection to the Creative Power within Humanity.

Right Now I Intend Joy.
Right Now I Feel Joy.
Right Now I Choose Joy.

I AM CREATING MY OWN FREEDOM

I Freely Choose Joy Right Now

I AM totally Free when I Consciously Choose my Connection within God. I hold the key to my Lasting Freedom through my ability to Consciously Choose Joy as my life Experience, no matter what appears to be.

The Only thing that ever binds me is my own negative energy Choices. No one else can Choose in my experience, and I cannot Choose for another. I may influence others (through their Choices alone), and I can allow others to influence me (by my Choices alone).

Other people, places, things, and experiences show up in ways that match my Creation Vibration. The entire world is a mirror upon which I view my thoughts and feelings in physical form. Whatever I believe, I receive. Whatever I decide, arrives.

My Lasting Freedom rests in my thoughts and feelings. No one does anything to me, that I have not thought about. If I never think a particular thing, I never experience that particular thing. My Contemplation of My World Creates My World.

LIFE ALLOWS ME TO EXPERIENCE MY BELIEFS

My Wisdom Is My Knowledge In Action

I AM Creating My Own Experience. All of my experiences Manifest because of my Attention. My Attention forms my Intention.

This entire book is only a bunch of concepts until they are experienced and Consciously used to Create my life. I AM the Only One Responsible for my Ability to Respond appropriately within my life experience.

My thoughts and feelings always ask for the continued Manifestation of similar thought and feeling experiences. I AM Responsible for my Choices.

God (Absolutely All of Life) Constantly and Consistently Manifests whatever I think and feel.

My experience of Joy (or not) in my life is God Giving Ongoing Direction reminding me that I AM Creating My Own Experience as I have envisioned it (by default or Decision).

There is no right or wrong way as I AM Creating My Own Experience. There is only what works to bring me Joy and a Connection with God (All of Life) or what doesn't work. I Consciously Choose all my thoughts and feelings that Connect me with God/Life/Energy.

I AM A JOYFUL BEING

I Intend Joy, I Feel Joy, And I Choose Joy

Anytime I feel anything other than Joy, I stop and I Consciously Intend Joy, Feel Joy, and Choose Joy. Anytime I think anything that denies my Joy and Potential, I stop and Consciously Intend Joy, Feel Joy, and Choose Joy. Only I can stop my emotionally guided opinions. Only I can Choose God Giving Ongoing Direction. Only I can Create in MY OWN life experience.

I Define my Joyous Life: I Define my Joyous Dreams with Crystal Clarity because I Create them. Every detail is important; only the details I want; only in the direction I wish to go; only to a good feeling level.

I Allow my Joyous Life: I Allow my dreams with ease and simplicity when I foster my Joy and Potential Always in All Ways. One Uplifting thought supports my Joy and Potential.

I Bring Joy to Life: I Bring Joy to my life by Intending Joy, Feeling Joy, and Choosing Joy.

Right Now
is the Only
Moment of Creation

Right Now
I Consciously Choose
My Creation Vibration

Right Now
I Choose Thoughts
that feel Good, that feel God

Right Now
I understand that
Life is set up for me to win

Right Now
When I feel Good
I AM letting my dreams in

ABOUT THE AUTHOR

Barry Thomas Bechta is an artist, author, and film maker whose work centers around the concepts of Unconditional Love. Barry knew he wanted to write from a very young age and was encouraged with his artistic skills and only began writing full time in his thirties. He wrote his first book, *I AM Creating My Own Experience* as a personal journal to choose connection with God/Life/Energy. He has since written 17 inspirational books.

Barry loves to hear from people whom have connected with his writing and used it as a tool to improve their lives. If you would like to write him about your personal experiences as a result of reading any of his books, Barry encourages you to do so.

You can also get a Free Digital Copy of *I AM Creating My Own Experience - The Creation Vibration* from his main website:

www.unconditionallovebooks.com

Unconditional Love Books Titles of Related Interest
by Barry Thomas Bechta

I AM Creating My Own Experience
978-0-9813485-5-1
I AM Creating My Own Answers
978-0-9686835-1-4
I AM Creating My Own Dreams
978-0-9686835-2-1
I AM Creating My Own Relationships
978-0-9686835-3-8
I AM Creating My Own Abundance
978-0-9686835-4-5
I AM Creating My Own Success
978-0-9686835-5-2
I AM Creating My Own Happiness
978-0-9686835-6-9
I AM Creating My Own Experience - The Creation Vibration
978-0-9686835-7-6
I AM Creating My Own Experience - To Manifest Money
978-0-9686835-8-3
I AM Creating My Own Experience - 369 Conscious Days
978-0-9686835-9-0
Loving Oneness
978-0-9813485-0-6
Trust Life
978-0-9813485-1-3
I AM Creating My Own Financial Freedom - The Story
978-0-9813485-2-0
I AM Creating My Own Financial Freedom - The Lessons
978-0-9813485-3-7
Laughing Star's Guide to Laughter, Life, Love, and God
978-0-9813485-4-4

All of the above are books are available through your local
bookstore, or they may be ordered as digital downloads at
www.unconditionallovebooks.com

Barry Thomas Bechta is available for interviews, special events, workshops, and lectures that redefine, guide, and inspire everyone's connection to the Creative Power within themselves. To arrange author interviews, special events, workshops, or lectures, please contact:

UNCONDITIONAL
LOVE BOOKS

Unconditional Love Books
Box # 610 - 2527 Pine St.,
Vancouver, BC, Canada V6J 3E8

info@unconditionallovebooks.com

www.unconditionallovebooks.com

For additional copies of Barry's books, products, and services please contact your local book seller. Many products and services are Only available to order directly from the publisher as eProducts on the website.

Thanks for your purchase and Remember to Consciously Create your Life.

Right Now is the Only Moment of Creation
Enjoy it Fully!

LaVergne, TN USA
10 January 2010
169490LV00001B/96/P